Daily DEVOTIONAL Prayer GUIDE

Revised Edition 2013

Rev. (Mrs) Funke Ewuosho

Daily Devotional Prayer

Copyright © 2013 by Rev. Funke Ewuosho

All rights reserved.

www.fowm.org

ISBN 978-0-9556597-4-4

All scripture quotations, unless otherwise indicated,
are taken from the Holy Bible: New King James Version (NKJV).
Copyright © 1982 by Thomas Nelson Inc.

Other translations used are Amplified Bible (AMP), The Message (MSG),
King James Version (KJV), New Living Translation (NLT)

Printed and bound in Great Britain by Book Printing UK
Remus House, Coltsfoot Drive, Peterborough, PE2 9BF

Cover Image: Flavio Takemoto

CONTENTS

Introduction to the Guide

When God said to Noah *'make yourself an ark'* (Genesis 6:14), that ark was to be for the salvation (deliverance and preservation) of his family from the flood that was to come upon the earth because of corruption. When the flood came, the only thing that wasn't submerged was the ark, but everything on the earth was destroyed except for the things and the people in the ark.

On the earth today, we have a deluge of sickness, diseases (curable and incurable), violence, perverted sex, corruption etc. True to God's Word in Isaiah 60:2, *"For behold, the darkness shall cover the earth and deep darkness the people"*; things might not get better on the earth but you can make an ark for yourself and your family.

One sure way to make that ark is by building a life of prayer. Prayer is not what we do only when we are in trouble, but as a lifestyle. The psalmist said his desire was to dwell in the house of the Lord all the days of his life;

In the desire to build an ark of safety through a lifestyle of prayer, God opened my eyes to the Lord's Prayer, which I have since then found to be very helpful. It is called the Lord's Prayer because Jesus Himself taught His disciples to pray in the manner. In Luke's account, it was in response to their request *"Lord, teach us to pray."* (Luke 11:1).

Jesus said to His disciples in Matthew 6:9 *"In this manner therefore pray."* I believe Jesus meant for it to be a pattern for prayer not just something to be rehearsed but to be developed. I have also found it to be a very comprehensive prayer pattern; it covers all areas - you can't miss anything out if you follow it.

In this guide, using it as a pattern, I have divided the Lord's Prayer into several prayer points and under each point you have quite a number of scriptural references that could guide your praying and also help build your faith in God as you pray.

This guide is also very flexible, in that you can use it in a short devotion (in which case you don't have to use all the scriptures) or in an extensive prayer time - the choice is yours. What matters is for you to commit to having a daily walk with God through prayer.

"Man shall not live by bread alone, but by every word that proceeds from the mouth of God." (Matthew 4:4). So, don't end your time of devotion without hearing God speak to

you by His Spirit and through His Word. Remember, one Word from God can change your life forever.

I therefore recommend a brief devotional Bible study after your praying.

God bless you,

Funke Ewuosho

Chapter 1

THANKSGIVING

Psalms 100

³ Know that the LORD, He *is* God;
It is He *who* has made us, and not we ourselves;
We are His people and the sheep of His pasture.
⁴ Enter into His gates with thanksgiving,
  And into His courts with praise.
Be thankful to Him, *and* bless His name.

Lamentations 3

²² *Through* the LORD's mercies we are not consumed,
Because His compassions fail not.
²³ *They are* new every morning;
Great *is* Your faithfulness.

Psalms 103

¹ Bless the LORD, O my soul;
And all that is within me, *bless* His holy name!
² Bless the LORD, O my soul,
And forget not all His benefits:

[3]Who forgives all your iniquities,
Who heals all your diseases,
[4]Who redeems your life from destruction,
Who crowns you with loving kindness and tender mercies,
[5]Who satisfies your mouth with good *things,*
So that your youth is renewed like the eagle's.

Psalms 89

[1]I will sing of the mercies of the LORD forever;
With my mouth will I make known Your faithfulness to all generations.

Chapter 2

THE LORD'S PRAYER PATTERN
(Matt. 6:9-13)

RELATIONSHIP AND WORSHIP

Our Father in heaven,
Hallowed be your name.
(Matt. 6:9)

John 4

[23] But the hour is coming, and now is, when the true worshipers will worship the Father in spirit and truth; for the Father is seeking such to worship Him [24] God *is* Spirit, and those who worship Him must worship in spirit and truth."

Ephesians 3

[14] For this reason I bow my knees to the Father of our Lord Jesus Christ, [15] from whom the whole family in heaven and earth is named,

Revelation 4

[8b] "I know your works. See, I have set before you
an open door, and no one can shut it; for you
have a little strength, have kept My word,
and have not denied My name.
[11] "You are worthy, O Lord,
To receive glory and honor and power;
For You created all things,
And by Your will they exist and were created."

Revelation 7

[12] saying:
"Amen! Blessing and glory and wisdom,
Thanksgiving and honor and power and might,
Be to our God forever and ever.
Amen."

Note: Our time of thanksgiving and worship can be enhanced
with songs of thanksgiving, praise and worship!

Chapter 3

PRAYER FOR THE NATIONS AND PERSONAL CONSECRATION

Your Kingdom come, Your will be done on
earth as it is in heaven.
(Matt. 6:10)

PRAY FOR THE NATIONS

Psalms 103

[19] The LORD has established His throne in heaven,
And His kingdom rules over all.

Daniel 2

[44] And in the days of these kings the God of heaven
will set up a kingdom which shall never be destroyed;
and the kingdom shall not be left to other people;
it shall break in pieces and consume all these kingdoms,
and it shall stand forever.

Daniel 4

[3] How great *are* His signs,
And how mighty His wonders!

His kingdom *is* an everlasting kingdom,
And His dominion *is* from generation to generation.

Numbers 14

²¹but truly, as I live, all the earth shall be filled #
With the glory of the LORD—

Habakkuk 2

¹⁴For the earth will be filled
With the knowledge of the glory of the LORD,
As the waters cover the sea.

Psalms 46

¹⁰Be still, and know that I *am* God;
I will be exalted among the nations,
I will be exalted in the earth!

Psalms 33

⁸Let all the earth fear the LORD;
Let all the inhabitants of the world stand in awe of Him.
⁹For He spoke, and it was *done;*
He commanded, and it stood fast.
¹⁰The LORD brings the counsel of the nations to nothing;
He makes the plans of the peoples of no effect.
¹¹The counsel of the LORD stands forever,
The plans of His heart to all generations.
¹²Blessed *is* the nation whose God *is* the LORD,
The people He has chosen as His own inheritance.

Daniel 4

[17b] In order that the living may know
That the Most High rules in the kingdom of men,
Gives it to whomever He will,
And sets over it the lowest of men.'

1 Timothy 2

[1] Therefore I exhort first of all that supplications,
prayers, intercessions, *and* giving of thanks be
made for all men, [2] for kings and all who are in
authority, that we may lead a quiet and peaceable
life in all godliness and reverence.

Revelations 5

[9b] "For You were slain,
And have redeemed us to God by Your blood
Out of every tribe and tongue and people and nation",

PERSONAL CONSECRATION

Romans 14

[17] for the kingdom of God is not eating and drinking,
but righteousness and peace and joy in the Holy Spirit.
[18] For he who serves Christ in these things *is* acceptable to
God and approved by men.

Luke 22

[42b] "….nevertheless not My will, but Yours, be done.

Philippians 2

[2] ....work out your own salvation with fear and trembling; [13] for it is God who works in you both to will and to do for *His* good pleasure.

Ephesians 2

[10] For we are His workmanship, created in Christ Jesus for good works, which God prepared beforehand that we should walk in them.

Philippians 3

[12] Not that I have already attained, or am already perfected; but I press on, that I may lay hold of that for which Christ Jesus has also laid hold of me.
[13] Brethren, I do not count myself to have apprehended; but one thing *I do,* forgetting those things which are behind and reaching forward to those things which are ahead,
[14] I press toward the goal for the prize of the upward call of God in Christ Jesus.

1 Corinthians 2

[9] But as it is written:
"Eye has not seen, nor ear heard,
Nor have entered into the heart of man
The things which God has prepared for those who love Him."
[10] But God has revealed *them* to us through His Spirit.
For the Spirit searches all things, yes, the deep things
Of God. [11] For what man knows the things of a man accept the spirit of the man which is in him? Even so no one knows the things of God except the Spirit of God.

[12] Now we have received, not the spirit of the world,
but the Spirit who is from God, that we might know the things
that have been freely given to us by God.

1 Thessalonians 5

[23] Now may the God of peace Himself sanctify you completely; and may your whole spirit, soul, and body be preserved blameless at the coming of our Lord Jesus Christ. [24] He who calls you *is* faithful, who also will do *it*.

2 Corinthians 3

[18] But we all, with unveiled face, beholding as in a mirror the glory of the Lord, are being transformed into the same image from glory to glory, just as by the Spirit of the Lord.

Chapter 4

PROVISION

Give us this day our daily bread.
(Matt. 6:11)

Matthew 6

[31] "Therefore do not worry, saying, 'What shall we eat?' or 'What shall we drink?' or What shall we wear?' [32] For after all these things the Gentiles seek. For your heavenly Father knows that you need all these things. [33] But seek first the kingdom of God and His righteousness, and all these things shall be added to you.

Matthew 7

[7] "Ask, and it will be given to you; seek, and you will find; knock, and it will be opened to you. [8] For everyone who asks receives, and he who seeks finds, and to him who knocks it will be opened. [9] Or what man is there among you who, if his son asks for bread, will give him a stone? [10] Or if he asks for a fish, will he give him a serpent? [11] If you then, being evil, know how to give good gifts to your children, how much more will your Father who is in heaven give good things to those who ask Him!

1 Peter 5

[7] casting all your care upon Him, for He cares
for you.

Psalm 84

[11] For the LORD God *is* a sun and shield; The LORD will give grace and glory; No good *thing* will He withhold from those who walk uprightly

Isaiah 1

[19] If you are willing and obedient, You shall eat the good of the land;

Deuteronomy 8

[18] "And you shall remember the LORD your God, for *it is* He who gives you power to get wealth, that He may establish His covenant which He swore to your fathers, as *it is* this day.

Psalms 23

[1] The LORD *is* my shepherd; I shall not want.

Psalms 103

[5] Who satisfies your mouth with good *things,*
So that your youth is renewed like the eagle's.

2 Corinthians 9

[8] And God *is* able to make all grace abound toward you, that you, always having all sufficiency in all *things,* may have an abundance for every good work.

Jeremiah 29

[11] For I know the thoughts that I think toward you, says the LORD, thoughts of peace and not of evil, to give you a future and a hope.

Chapter 5

REPENTANCE AND FORGIVENESS OF SINS

And forgive us our debts, as we forgive our debtors.
(Matt. 6:12)

Mark 11

[23] For assuredly, I say to you, whoever says to this mountain, Be removed and be cast into the sea,' and does not doubt in his heart, but believes that those things he says will be done, he will have whatever he says. [25] "And whenever you stand praying, if you have anything against anyone, forgive him, that your Father in heaven may also forgive you your trespasses.

Matthew 6

[14] "For if you forgive men their trespasses, your heavenly Father will also forgive you. [15] But if you do not forgive men their trespasses, neither will your Father forgive your trespasses.

Matthew 5

[44] But I say to you, love your enemies, bless those who curse you,

do good to those who hate you, and pray for those who spitefully use you and persecute you,

1 Corinthians 13

5 loves does not behave rudely, does not seek its own, is not provoked, and thinks no evil;

Romans 12

17 Repay no one evil for evil. Have regard for good things in the sight of all men. 18 If it is possible, as much as depends on you, live peaceably with all men. 19 Beloved, do not avenge yourselves, but *rather* give place to wrath; for it is written, "Vengeance *is* Mine, I will repay," says the Lord. 20 Therefore "If your enemy is hungry, feed him; If he is thirsty, give him a drink; For in so doing you will heap coals of fire on his head."

1 John 1

9 If we confess our sins, He is faithful and just to forgive us *our* sins and to cleanse us from all unrighteousness.

Hebrews 4

15 For we do not have a High Priest who cannot sympathize with our weaknesses, but was in all *points* tempted as *we are, yet* without sin.
16 Let us therefore come boldly to the throne of grace that we may obtain mercy and find grace to help in time of need.

Chapter 6

PROTECTION AND DELIVERANCE

And do not lead us into temptation, but deliver us from
the evil one.
(Matt. 6:13)

Luke 22
[40] "...Pray that you may not enter into temptation."

2 Peter 2
[9] *then* the Lord knows how to deliver the godly out of
temptations and to reserve the unjust under punishment for the
day of judgment,

1 Corinthians 10
[13] No temptation has overtaken you except such as is
common to man; but God *is* faithful, who will not allow you to be
tempted beyond what you are able, but with the temptation will
also make the way of escape, that you may be able to bear *it*.

Hebrews 2
[18] For in that He Himself has suffered, being tempted, He is able to
aid those who are tempted.

Psalms 91

[1]He who dwells in the secret place of the Most High
Shall abide under the shadow of the Almighty.
[2]I will say of the LORD, *"He is* my refuge and my fortress;
My God, in Him I will trust."
[3]Surely He shall deliver you from the snare of the fowler[1]
And from the perilous pestilence.
[4]He shall cover you with His feathers,
And under His wings you shall take refuge;
His truth *shall be your* shield and buckler.
[5]You shall not be afraid of the terror by night,
or of the arrow *that* flies by day,
[6]*Nor* of the pestilence *that* walks in darkness,
Nor of the destruction *that* lays waste at noonday.
[7]A thousand may fall at your side, And ten thousand at
your right hand; *But* it shall not come near you.
[8]Only with your eyes shall you look,
And see the reward of the wicked.
[9]Because you have made the LORD, *who is* my refuge,
Even the Most High, your dwelling place,
[10]No evil shall befall you,
Nor shall any plague come near your dwelling;
[11]For He shall give His angels charge over you,
To keep you in all your ways.
[12]In *their* hands they shall bear you up,
Lest you dash your foot against a stone.
[13]You shall tread upon the lion and the cobra,
The young lion and the serpent you shall trample underfoot.
[14]"Because he has set his love upon Me, therefore I will deliver
him; I will set him on high, because he has known My name.
[15]He shall call upon Me, and I will answer him;

I *will be* with him in trouble;
I will deliver him and honour him.
[16] With long life I will satisfy him,
And show him My salvation."

Proverbs 18

[10] The name of the LORD *is* a strong tower;
The righteous run to it and are safe.

Colossians 3

[3] For you died, and your life is hidden with Christ
in God.

Psalms 17

[8] Keep me as the apple of Your eye;
       Hide me under the shadow of Your wings,

Isaiah 54

[14] In righteousness you shall be established;
You shall be far from oppression, for you shall not fear;
And from terror, for it shall not come near you.
[15] Indeed they shall surely assemble, *but* not because of Me.
Whoever assembles against you shall fall for your sake.
[16] "Behold, I have created the blacksmith
Who blows the coals in the fire,
Who brings forth an instrument for his work;
And I have created the spoiler to destroy.
[17] No weapon formed against you shall prosper,
And every tongue *which* rises against you in judgment
You shall condemn.

This *is* the heritage of the servants of the LORD,
And their righteousness *is* from Me,"
Says the LORD.

Psalms 34

¹⁹ Many *are* the afflictions of the righteous,
But the LORD delivers him out of them all.
²⁰ He guards all his bones;
Not one of them is broken.

John 10

¹⁰ The thief does not come except to steal, and to kill, and to destroy. I have come that they may have life, and that they may have *it* more abundantly.

Isaiah 53

⁴ Surely He has borne our griefs (Sickness)
And carried our sorrows (pains)...
⁵ ...The chastisement for our peace *was* upon Him, And by His stripes we are healed.

Matthew 8

¹⁷ "...He Himself took our infirmities
And bore our sicknesses."

Psalm 23

⁴ Yea, though I walk through the valley of the
shadow of death, I will fear no evil;
For You *are* with me; Your rod and Your staff, they comfort me.

[5]You prepare a table before me in the presence of my enemies; You anoint my head with oil;
My cup runs over.
[6]Surely goodness and mercy shall follow me
All the days of my life;
And I will dwell in the house of the LORD Forever.

Psalm 121

[1]I will lift up my eyes to the hills—
From whence comes my help?
[2]My help *comes* from the LORD,
Who made heaven and earth.
[3]He will not allow your foot to be moved;
He who keeps you will not slumber.
[4]Behold, He who keeps Israel
Shall neither slumber nor sleep.
[5]The LORD *is* your keeper;
The LORD *is* your shade at your right hand.
[6]The sun shall not strike you by day,
Nor the moon by night.
[7]The LORD shall preserve you from all evil;
He shall preserve your soul.
[8]The LORD shall preserve your going out and your coming in
From this time forth, and even forevermore.

Psalm 125

[1]Those who trust in the LORD
Are like Mount Zion,
Which cannot be moved, *but* abides forever.
[2]As the mountains surround Jerusalem,

So the LORD surrounds His people
From this time forth and forever.

Isaiah 10

²⁷It shall come to pass in that day
That his burden will be taken away from your shoulder,
And his yoke from your neck,
And the yoke will be destroyed because of the anointing oil.

James 4

⁷Therefore submit to God. Resist the devil and he will flee from you.

Matthew 16

¹⁹And I will give you the keys of the kingdom of heaven, and whatever you bind on earth will be bound in heaven, and whatever you loose on earth will be loosed in heaven."

Chapter 7

PRAY FOR YOUR FAMILY
& LOVED ONES

SALVATION OF THEIR SOULS

Acts 16

[31] So they said, "Believe on the Lord Jesus Christ, and you will be saved, you and your household."

Joel 2

[28] "And it shall come to pass afterward That I will pour out My Spirit on all flesh;

Your sons and your daughters shall prophesy,

Your old men shall dream dreams, Your young men shall see visions.

2 Corinthians 4

[3] But even if our gospel is veiled, it is veiled to those who are perishing, [4] whose minds the god of this age has blinded, who do not believe, lest the light of the gospel of the glory of Christ, who is the image of God, should shine on them.

Matthew 12

29 Or how can one enter a strong man's house and plunder his goods, unless he first binds the strong man? And then he will plunder his house.

Matthew 16

19 And I will give you the keys of the kingdom of heaven, and whatever you bind on earth will be bound in heaven, and whatever you loose on earth will be loosed in heaven."

1 John 3

8 He who sins is of the devil, for the devil has sinned from the beginning. For this purpose the Son of God was manifested, that He might destroy the works of the devil.

2 Corinthians 10

3 For though we walk in the flesh, we do not war according to the flesh. 4 For the weapons of our warfare *are* not carnal but mighty in God for pulling down strongholds, 5 casting down arguments and every high thing that exalts itself against the knowledge of God, bringing every thought into captivity to the obedience of Christ,

Isaiah 54

13 All your children *shall be* taught by the LORD,
And great *shall be* the peace of your children.

Titus 2

[11] For the grace of God that brings salvation has appeared to all men, [12] teaching us that, denying ungodliness and worldly lusts, we should live soberly, righteously, and godly in the present age,

Isaiah 49

[25] But thus says the Lord:
"Even the captives of the mighty shall be taken away,
And the prey of the terrible be delivered;
For I will contend with him who contends with you,
And I will save your children.

Chapter 8

PRAYER FOR PARTNERS OF FOWM

Philippians 1

[2] Grace to you and peace from God our Father and the Lord Jesus Christ. [3] I thank my God upon every remembrance of you, [4] always in every prayer of mine making request for you all with joy, [5] for your fellowship in the gospel from the first day until now, [6] being confident of this very thing, that He who has begun a good work in you will complete *it* until the day of Jesus Christ; [7] just as it is right for me to think this of you all, because I have you in my heart, inasmuch as both in my chains and in the defence and confirmation of the gospel, you all are partakers with me of grace.

Philippians 4

[19] And my God shall supply all your need according to His riches in glory by Christ Jesus.

Luke 6

[8] Give, and it will be given to you: good measure, pressed down, shaken together, and running over will be put into your bosom.

For with the same measure that you use, it will be measured back to you."

Mark 10
[29] So Jesus answered and said, "Assuredly, I say to you, there is no one who has left house or brothers or sisters or father or mother or wife or children or lands, for My sake and the gospel's, [30] who shall not receive a hundred fold now in this time—houses and brothers and sisters and mothers and children and lands, with Persecutions and in the age to come, eternal life.

Malachi 3
[10] Bring all the tithes into the storehouse,
That there may be food in My house,
And try Me now in this,"
Says the LORD of hosts,
"If I will not open for you the windows of heaven
And pour out for you *such* blessing
That *there will* not *be room* enough *to receive it.* [11] "And I will re-buke the devourer for your sakes,
So that he will not destroy the fruit of your ground,
Nor shall the vine fail to bear fruit for you in the field,"
Says the LORD of hosts;
[12] "And all nations will call you blessed,
For you will be a delightful land,"
Says the LORD of hosts.

Numbers 6
[24] "The LORD bless you and keep you;
[25] The LORD make His face shine upon you,
And be gracious to you;

²⁶ The LORD lift up His countenance upon you,
And give you peace."'

Deuteronomy 28

³ "Blessed *shall* you *be* in the city, and blessed *shall* you *be* in the country.
⁴ "Blessed *shall be* the fruit of your body, the produce of your ground
⁶ "Blessed *shall* you *be* when you come in, and blessed *shall* you *be* when you go out.
⁷ "The LORD will cause your enemies who rise against you to be defeated before your face; they shall come out against you one way and flee before you seven ways.
⁸ "The LORD will command the blessing on you in your storehouses and in all to which you set your hand, and He will bless you in the land which the LORD your God is giving you.
⁹ "The LORD will establish you as a holy (Special) people to Himself,
¹¹ And the LORD will grant you plenty of goods,
¹² The LORD will open to you His good treasure, the heavens, to give the rain to your land in its season, and to bless all the work of your hand. You shall lend to many nations, but you shall not borrow.
¹³ And the LORD will make you the head and not the tail; you shall be above only, and not be beneath

2 Corinthians 8

⁹ For you know the grace of our Lord Jesus Christ, that though He was rich, yet for your sakes He became poor, that you through His poverty might become rich.

2 Corinthians 9

8And God *is* able to make all grace abound toward you, that you, always having all sufficiency in all *things,* may have an abundance for every good work.

3 John

2Beloved, I pray that you may prosper in all things and be in health, just as your soul prospers.

Ephesians 1

17that the God of our Lord Jesus Christ, the Father of glory, may give to you the spirit of wisdom and revelation in the knowledge of Him,
18the eyes of your understanding being enlightened; that you may know what is the hope of His calling, what are the riches of the glory of His inheritance in the saints,
19and what *is* the exceeding greatness of His power toward us who believe, according to the working of His mighty power

Colossians 1

9For this reason we also, since the day we heard it, do not cease to pray for you, and to ask that you may be filled with the knowledge of His will in all wisdom and spiritual understanding;
10that you may walk worthy of the Lord, fully pleasing *Him,* being fruitful in every good work and increasing in the knowledge of God;
11strengthened with all might, according to His glorious power, for all patience and longsuffering with joy;

[12] giving thanks to the Father who has qualified us to be partakers of the inheritance of the saints in the light.

Psalm 138

[8] The LORD will perfect *that which* concerns me;
Your mercy, O LORD, *endures* forever;
Do not forsake the works of Your hands.

Colossians 4

[12] ...Always labouring fervently for you in prayers, that you may stand perfect and complete in all the will of God.

Chapter 9

COMMIT YOUR DAY INTO GOD'S HANDS

Psalm 118

[24] This *is* the day the LORD has made;
We will rejoice and be glad in it.

Psalm 139

[16] Your eyes saw my substance, being yet unformed.
And in Your book they all were written,
The days fashioned for me,
When *as yet there were* none of them.

Psalm 37

[5] Commit your way to the LORD,
Trust also in Him,
And He shall bring *it* to pass.
[23] The steps of a *good* man are ordered by the LORD,
And He delights in his way.
[24] Though he fall, he shall not be utterly cast down;
For the LORD upholds *him with* His hand.

Proverbs 3

⁵Trust in the LORD with all your heart,
And lean not on your own understanding;
⁶In all your ways acknowledge Him,
And He shall direct your paths.

Romans 8

²⁸And we know that all things work together
for good to those who love God,
to those who are the called according to *His* purpose.

2 Corinthians 2

¹⁴Now thanks *be* to God who always leads us in triumph
in Christ,
and through us diffuses the fragrance of His knowledge in every
place.

Psalm 1

¹Blessed *is* the man
Who walks not in the counsel of the ungodly,
Nor stands in the path of sinners,
Nor sits in the seat of the scornful;
²But his delight *is* in the law of the LORD,
And in His law he meditates day and night.
³He shall be like a tree
Planted by the rivers of water,
That brings forth its fruit in its season,
Whose leaf also shall not wither;
And whatever he does shall prosper.

Psalm 16

[5] O LORD, *You are* the portion of my inheritance
and my cup; You maintain my lot.
[6] The lines have fallen to me in pleasant *places;*
Yes, I have a good inheritance.

Psalm 68

[28] Your God has commanded your strength;
Strengthen, O God, what You have done for us.

Chapter 10

GIVE THANKS FOR ANSWERS TO YOUR PRAYERS

Psalm 65

[2] O You who hear prayer,
To You all flesh will come.

Psalm 34

[17] *The righteous* cry out, and the LORD hears,
And delivers them out of all their troubles.

Mark 11

[11] And Jesus went into Jerusalem and into the temple. So when He had looked around at all things, as the hour was already late, He went out to Bethany with the twelve.

Ephesians 3

[20] Now to Him who is able to do exceedingly abundantly above all that we ask or think, according to the power that works in us,

Philippians 4

[6]Be anxious for nothing, but in everything by prayer and supplication, with thanksgiving, let your requests be made known to God;

Chapter 11

DECLARATION

For Yours is the Kingdom and the power and the glory
forever. Amen.
(Matt. 6:13)

Revelation 5
[13] "Blessing and honour and glory and power
Be to Him who sits on the throne,
And to the Lamb, forever and ever!"

Revelation 11
[15] " ...The kingdoms of this world have become the kingdoms of our
Lord and of His Christ, and He shall reign forever and ever!"

APPENDIX

Intercessory Prayer Guide

I.

PURPOSE:

To move from the Outer Court, through the Inner Court into the Holy of Holies, i.e. God's presence to do business with Him in prayer.

COME INTO HIS GATES WITH THANKSGIVING & HIS COURTS WITH PRAISE.

'Enter His gates with thanksgiving and into His courts with praise; give thanks to Him and praise His name.' (Ps. 100:4).

CONFESS OUR SINS & REPENT BEFORE HIM. ASK AND RECEIVE HIS FORGIVENESS AND CLEANSING FOR ALL UNRIGHTEOUSNESS.

(As priests, we should also intercede for the sins of others to be forgiven)

'Surely the arm of the Lord is not too short to save, nor His ear too dull to hear. But your iniquities have separated you from your God; your sins have hidden His face from you, so that He will not hear..' (Is. 59:1-2).

Therefore confess your sins to each other and pray for each other so that you may be healed. The prayer of a righteous man is powerful and effective.' (Jas. 5:16).

'If we confess our sins, He is faithful and just to forgive us our sins and to cleanse us from all unrighteousness.' (1 Jn. 1:9).

ASK FOR & RECEIVE THE HELP OF THE HOLY SPIRIT IN PRAYER.

'Trust in the Lord with all your heart and lean not on your own understanding; in all your ways acknowledge Him, and He will make your path straight' (Pr. 3:5-6).

'Commit your way to the Lord, trust in Him and He will do this: He will make your righteousness shine like the dawn, the justice of your cause like the noonday sun.' (Ps. 37:5-6).

'In the same way, the Spirit helps us in our weakness. We do not know what we ought to pray. But the Spirit Himself intercedes for us with groans that words cannot express. And He who searches our hearts knows the mind of the Spirit, because the Spirit intercedes for the saints in accordance with God's will.' (Rom. 8:26-27).

'Pray in the Spirit on all occasions with this in mind, be alert and always keep on praying for all the saints' (Eph. 3:16).

CHARGE YOURSELF UP SO AS TO BE SENSITIVE TO, AND FLOW WITH THE HOLY SPIRIT & BE STRENGTHENED UNTO PRAYER.

'He who speaks in a tongue edifies himself' (1 Cor. 14:4).

'Build yourselves up in your most holy faith and pray in the Holy Spirit' (Jude 20).

II.

NOW THAT WE ARE IN THE SPIRIT, LET'S START BY WORSHIPPING GOD IN SPIRIT & IN TRUTH.

'God is spirit, and His worshippers must worship in spirit and in truth' (Jn. 4:24).

'This is how you should pray: Our Father in heaven, hallowed by your name.' (Matt. 6:9).

PRAYER POINTS

THE AREA, THE NATION & THE NATIONS

'Your kingdom come, Your will be done on earth as it is in heaven' (Matt. 6:10).

'And I will build my church, and the gates of Hades will not overcome it. I will give you the keys of the kingdom of heaven; whatever you bind on earth will be bound in heaven, and whatever you loose on earth will be loosed in heaven.' (Matt. 16:18-19).

'I tell you the truth, whatever you bind on earth will be bound in heaven, and whatever you loose on earth will be loosed in heaven. Again I tell you that if two of you on earth agree about anything you ask for, it will be done for you by my Father in heaven. For where two or three come together in my name, there am I with them.' (Matt. 18:18-20).

'the prayer of a righteous man is powerful and effective. Elijah was a man just like us. He prayed earnestly that it would not rain, and it did not rain on the land for three and a half years. Again he prayed, and the heavens gave rain, and the earth produced its crops.' (Jas. 5:16b-18).

'The earth is the Lord's, and everything in it, the world, and all who live in it.' (Ps. 24:1).

Pray for the outpouring of His Spirit, that will bring about salvation and all of God's will to be done in the land & in the lives of people and the nations & for righteousness to be restored.

'And afterwards, I will pour out my Spirit on all people. Your sons and daughters will prophesy, your old men will dream dreams, your young men will see visions. Even on my servants, both men and women. I will pour out my spirit in those days. I will show wonders in the heavens and on the earth.' (Joel 2:28-30a).

'till the Spirit is poured upon us from on high, and the desert becomes a fertile field, and the fertile field seems like a forest. Justice will dwell in the desert and righteousness live in the fertile field. The fruit of righteousness will be peace; the effect of righteousness will be quietness and confidence forever. My people will live in peaceful dwelling-places, in secure homes, in undisturbed places of rest.' (Isa. 32:15-18).

'Your people will rebuild the ancient ruins and will raise up the age-old foundations; you will be called repairer of Broken Walls, Restorer of streets with Dwellings.' (Isa. 58:12).

'I urge then, first of all, that requests, prayers, intercession and thanksgiving be made for everyone- for kings and all those in authority, that we may live peaceful and quiet lives in all godliness and holiness. This is good, and pleases God our Saviour, who wants all men to be saved and to come to a knowledge of the truth.' (1 Tim. 2:1-4).

'For the earth to be filled with the knowledge of the Lord as the waters cover the sea.' (Isa. 11:9).

Pray that people's minds be opened to receive & to believe the gospel.

'The god of this age has blinded the minds of unbelievers, so that they cannot see the light of the gospel of the glory of Christ, who is the image of God.' (2 Cor. 4:4).

Demolish strongholds, reasonings, high things exalted above the knowledge of God in their minds, take every thought captive & make it obedient to Christ.

'For though we live in the world, we do not wage war as the world does. The weapons we fight with are not the weapons of the world. On the contrary, they have divine power to demolish strongholds. We demolish arguments and every pretension that sets itself up against the knowledge of God, and we make it obedient to Christ.' (2 Cor. 10:3-5).

Loose the people from Satan's bondage (to sin) and to come to be saved.

'The Spirit of the Lord is on me, because He has anointed me to preach good news to the poor. He has sent me to proclaim freedom for the prisoners, and recovery of sight for the blind, to release the oppressed, to proclaim the year of the Lord's favour.' (Lk. 4:18).

THE CHURCH OF JESUS CHRIST IN THE AREA, THE UK & IN THE NATIONS

'I will build my church and the gates of Hades (hell) will not overcome it (or not prove stronger than it).' (Matt. 16:18).

'Arise, shine, for your light has come, and the glory of the Lord rises upon you. See, darkness covers the earth and thick darkness is over the peoples, but the Lord rises upon you and His glory appears over you. Nations will come to your light and kings to the brightness of your dawn.' (Isa. 60:1-3).

'For Zion's sake I will not keep silent, for Jerusalem's sake I will not remain quiet, till her righteousness shines out like the dawn, her salvation like a blazing torch. The nations will see your right-eousness and all the kings your glory; you will be called by a new name that the mouth of the Lord will bestow. You will be a crown of splendour in the Lord's hand, a royal diadem in the hand of your God....the Lord will take delight in you, and your land will be married. As a young man marries a maiden, so will your sons marry you; as a bridegroom rejoices over his bride, so will your God rejoice over you. I have posted watchmen on your walls, O Jerusalem; they will never be silent day or night. You who call on the Lord, give yourselves no rest.' (Isa. 62:1-6).

'Holy father, protect them by the power of Your name- the name You gave Me- so that they may be one as We are one.' (John 17:11).

THE LEADERSHIP OF THE CHURCH (MINISTERS OF THE GOSPEL)

To be focused on God in Prayer & the ministry of the Word.

'give our attention to prayer and the ministry of the word.' (Acts 6:4).

To be united in spirit and in purpose, through humility and maturity.

'They all joined together constantly in prayer, along with the women and Mary the mother of Jesus, and his brothers.' (Acts 1:14).

'then Peter stood up with the Eleven, raised his voice and addressed the crowd.' (Acts 2:14).

For boldness & courage to declare the word of God.

'Pray also for me, that whenever I open my mouth, words may be given me so that I will fearlessly make known the mystery of the Gospel, for which I am an ambassador in chains. Pray that I may declare it fearlessly, as I should.' (Eph. 6:19-20).

'Now Lord, consider their threats and enable Your servants to speak Your word with great boldness. Stretch out Your hand to heal and perform miraculous signs and wonders through the name of Your holy servant Jesus.' (Acts 4:29-30).

'I am not ashamed of the Gospel, because it is the power of God for the salvation of everyone who believes.' (Rom. 1:16).

Ask for God's Protection & Deliverance for them & their families.

'Strike the shepherd, and the sheep will be scattered...' (Zech. 13:7).

'It was about this time that King Herod arrested some who belonged to the church, intending to persecute them. He had James, the brother of John, put to death with the sword. When he saw that this pleased the Jews, he proceeded to seize Peter also. This happened during the Feast of Unleavened Bread. After arresting him, he put him in prison, handing him over to be guarded by four squads of four soldiers each. Herod intended to bring him out for public trial after the Passover. So Peter was kept in prison, but the church was earnestly praying to God for him.' (Acts 12:1-5).

'Finally, brothers, pray for us that the message of the Lord may spread rapidly and be honoured, just as it was with you. And pray that we may be delivered from wicked and evil men.' (2 Thess. 3:1-2).

Pray that God will raise other levels of leadership that will share the burden with them.

'In those days when the number of disciples was increasing,....the Twelve gathered all the disciples together and said: It would not be right for us to neglect the ministry of the word of God in order to wait on tables. Brothers, choose seven men from among you who are known to be full of the Spirit and wisdom. We will turn this responsibility over to them and will give our attention to prayer and the ministry of the word.... They presented these men to the apostles, who prayed and laid their hands on them. So the word of God spread. The number of disciples increased rapidly, and a large number of priests became obedient to the faith.' (Acts 6:1-7).

'the Amalekites came and attacked the Israelites at Rephidim. Moses said to Joshua: Choose some of our men and go out to fight the Amalekites. Tomorrow I will stand on the top of the hill with the staff of God in my hands. So Joshua fought the Amalekites as Moses had ordered, and Moses, Aaron and Hur went to the top of the hill. As long as Moses help up his hands, the Israelites were winning...Aaron and Hur held his hands up that his hands remained steady till sunset. So Joshua overcame the Amalekite army with the sword.' (Ex. 17:8-13).

'It was He who gave some to be apostles, some to be prophets, some to be evangelists, and some to be pastors and teachers, to prepare God's people for works of service, so that the body of Christ may be built up.' (Eph. 4:11-12).

MEMBERS OF THE BODY OF CHRIST

'To be granted the spirit of wisdom and revelation, so that we may know Him better, and the hope of His calling and the riches of His glorious inheritance in the saints and His incomparably great
power towards us who believe.' (Eph. 1:15-23).

For us to be strengthened with power by the Holy Spirit in the inner man, to be rooted & established in his love... (Eph. 3:14-21).

'Be strong in the Lord and in His mighty power.' (Eph. 6:10).

'To be filled with the knowledge of God's will in all wisdom & spiritual understanding, that we may live a life worthy of Him, being pleasing unto him & fruitful in every good work.' (Col. 1:9-14). 'You are the salt of the earth...You are the light of the world. A city on a hill cannot be hidden...Let your light shine before men, that they may see your good deeds and praise your Father in heaven.' (Matt. 5:13-16).

To grow up into Christ in all things, that we no longer remain as children.

'...the body of Christ may be built up until we all reach unity in the faith and in the knowledge of the Son of God and become mature...speaking the truth in love, we will in all things grow up into Him who is the head.' (Eph. 4:12-16).

'Anyone who live on milk being still an infant, is not acquainted with the teaching about righteousness. But the solid food is for the mature, who by constant use have trained themselves to distinguish good from evil.' (Heb. 5:11-14).

To yield to the inner working of God - 'For it is God who works in you both to will (desire) and to act according to His good purpose.' (Php. 2:13).

'Live by the Spirit, and you will not gratify the desires of the sinful nature.' (Gal. 5:16).

To do the works of ministry. 'To prepare God's people for works of service, so the body of Christ may be built up.' (Eph. 4:12).

'Those who had been scattered (i.e. the disciples) preached the word wherever they went.' (Acts 8:4).

'Ask the Lord of the harvest, therefore to send out workers into His harvest field.' (Lk. 10:2).

'The Spirit of the Lord is on me, because He anointed me to preach good news' (Lk. 4:18).

'...and how can they hear without someone preaching to them?' (Rom. 10:14b).

To walk in love and unity of the Spirit

'How good and pleasant it is when brothers live together in unity.' (Ps. 133:1).

'Let us love one another, for love comes from God. Everyone who loves has been born of God and knows God. Whoever does not love does not know God, because God is love.' (1 Jn. 4:7-8).

To walk in victory in every area of our lives

'For everyone born of God overcomes the world. This is the victory that has overcome the world, even our faith... he who believes that Jesus is the Son of God.' (1 Jn. 5:4-5).

'He is able to do immeasurably more than all we ask or imagine, according to His power that is at work within us.' (Eph. 3:20).

'My God will meet all your needs according to His glorious riches in Christ Jesus.' (Php. 4:19).

'You know the grace of our Lord Jesus Christ, that though He was rich, yet for your sakes He became poor, so that you through His poverty might become rich.' (2 Cor. 8:9).

'God is able to make all grace abound to you, so that in all things, at all times, having all that you need, you will abound in every good work.' (2 Cor. 9:8).

FOR THE CHURCH SERVICE

For a revelation and the manifestation of the power and glory of God, bringing salvation, healing, deliverance and effecting God's will and purpose for the meeting.

'God, You are my God, earnestly I seek You; my soul thirsts for You. I have seen You in the sanctuary and beheld Your power and Your Glory.' (Ps. 63:1-2).

For the anointing to rest on the worship, word and ministry and every facet of the service.

'You have exalted my horn like that of a wild ox; fine oils have been poured upon me.' (Ps. 92:10).

For Jesus to be Lord indeed and the Holy Spirit to be in control throughout, and everyone being in total alignment with Him. That there will be agreement in the house.

'How good and pleasant it is when brothers live together in unity.

It is like precious oil poured on the head, running down on the beard, running down on Aaron's beard, down up on the collar of his robes. It is as if the dew of Hermon were falling on Mount Zion. For there the Lord bestows His blessing, even life forever-more.' (Ps. 133).

For a fresh anointing upon the worship team, the preacher & ministry team and the congregation.

'Now the Lord is Spirit, and where the Spirit of the Lord is, there is freedom.' (2 Cor. 3:17).

That souls be saved and believers built up and equipped.

'...as He was teaching.... the power of the Lord was present for Him to heal the sick' (Lk. 5:17).

'In that day, their burden will be lifted from your shoulders, their yoke from your neck; the yoke will be broken....' (Isa. 10:27).

Recommended Products

To help you to develop your prayer life, we encourage you to order some of these related book and messages by Rev. Funke Ewuosho.

- **The Art of Prayer and Worship**

- **The Prayer Series**

- **Kingdom Power Praying**

- **Speaking the Blessing**

- **Confession Brings Possession**

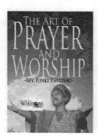   

Become a FOWM Partner

If you have been blessed by this material we would love to hear from you. Please contact one of our offices or visit www.fowm.org for details and we will send you regular emails, teaching materials and further information about partnership with the Ministry.

Visit our website **www.fowm.org** to read our online teaching messages, watch video messages, submit your prayer requests and purchase life-changing products.

Other Recommended Titles

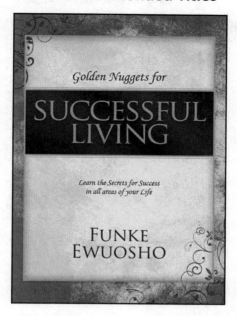

Golden Nuggets for Successful Living
Funke Ewuosho

Most people desire to be successful, but how many of us are applying the right principles to actually experience success in all areas of our lives? God's Word is a handbook for life, loaded with the wisdom we need to succeed. This book, Golden Nuggets For Successful Living, is a compilation of teachings by Rev. Funke Ewuosho covering five major areas: Personal Development; Leadership; Family; Relationships and Tools for Successful Living. It contains many wisdom nuggets to enhance you in all areas of your life - mentally, socially, physically and, most importantly - spiritually! *"And Jesus increased in wisdom and stature, and in favor with God and men." (Lk. 2:52).*

Other Recommended Titles

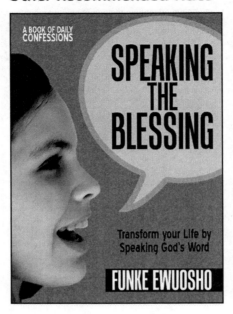

Speaking the Blessing
Funke Ewuosho

Did you know that you can change your life by changing your
confession? God's blessing has been made available to
every one of us but whether we will experience it is
another matter! Speaking God's Word over our lives
on a regular basis will enable us to walk in the reality of
the blessing. This powerful book of Scripture confessions
will help you to get started on the road to experiencing
transformation in every area of your life.

ISBN: 978-0-9556597-3-7